Draw TRANSPORT
Victor Gibbs

Series Editors: David and Brenda Herbert

A & C BLACK · LONDON

First published 1982
Reprinted 1985
by A & C Black (Publishers) Ltd
35 Bedford Row, London WC1R 4JH

ISBN 0-7136-2192-3

© A & C Black (Publishers) Ltd 1982

All rights reserved. No part of this publication may be
reproduced, stored in a retrieval system, or
transmitted, in any form or by any means, electronic,
mechanical, photocopying, recording or otherwise,
without the prior permission in writing of
A & C Black (Publishers) Ltd

Printed in Great Britain by
Whitstable Litho Ltd., Whitstable, Kent

Contents

Making a start

Learning to draw is largely a matter of practice and observation — so draw as much and as often as you can, and use your eyes all the time.

Look around you — at chairs, tables, plants, people, pets, buildings, your hand holding this book. Everything is worth drawing. The time you spend on a drawing is not important. A ten-minute sketch can say more than a slow, painstaking drawing that takes many hours.

Carry a sketchbook with you whenever possible, and don't be shy of using it in public, either for quick notes to be used later or for a finished drawing.

To do an interesting drawing, you must enjoy it. Even if you start on something that doesn't particularly interest you, you will probably find that the act of drawing it — and looking at it in a new way — creates its own excitement. The less you think about how you are drawing and the more you think about what you are drawing, the better your drawing will be.

The best equipment will not itself make you a better artist — a masterpiece can be drawn with a stump of pencil on a scrap of paper. But good equipment is encouraging and pleasant to use, so buy the best you can afford and don't be afraid to use it freely.

Be as bold as you dare. It's your piece of paper and you can do what you like with it. Experiment with the biggest piece of paper and the boldest, softest piece of chalk or crayon you can find, filling the paper with lines — scribbles, funny faces, lettering, anything — to get a feeling of freedom. Even if you think you have a gift for tiny delicate line drawings with a fine pen or pencil, this is worth trying. It will act as a 'loosening up' exercise. The results may surprise you.

Be self-critical. If a drawing looks wrong scrap it and start again. A second, third or even fourth attempt will often be better than the first, because you are learning more about the subject all the time. Use an eraser as little as possible — piecemeal correction won't help. Don't re-trace your lines. If a line is right the first time, leave it alone — heavier re-drawing leads to a dull, mechanical look.

Try drawing in colour. Dark blue, reddish-brown and dark green are good drawing colours. A coloured pencil, pen or chalk can often be very useful for detail, emphasis or contrast on a black and white drawing: for instance, in a street scene, draw the buildings in black, the people, cars etc. in another colour. This simple technique can be very effective.

You can learn a lot from looking at other people's drawings. But you will learn more from a drawing done from direct observation of the subject or even out of your head, however stiff and unsatisfactory the results may seem at first.

A lot can be learned by practice and from books, but a teacher can be a great help. If you get the chance, don't hesitate to join a class — even one evening a week can do a lot of good.

What to draw with

Pencils are graded according to hardness, from 6H (the hardest) through 5H, 4H, 3H, 2H to H; then HB; then B, through 1B, 2B, 3B, 4B, 5B up to 6B (the softest). For most purposes, a soft pencil (HB or softer) is best. If you keep it sharp, it will draw as fine a line as a hard pencil but with less pressure, which makes it easier to control. Sometimes it is effective to smudge the line with your finger or an eraser, but if you do this too much the drawing will look woolly. Pencil is the most versatile of all drawing techniques, suitable for anything from the most precise linear drawing to broad tonal treatment. Of course, a pencil line, even at its heaviest, is never a true black. But it has a lustrous, pewtery quality that is very attractive.

Charcoal can be bought in various qualities and sizes. I advise short sticks since they are cheaper, and long sticks soon break into short sticks anyhow.

Charcoal (which is soft and crumbly) is ideal for bold, large drawings. But beware of accidental smudging. Never rest your hand on the paper as you draw. If you are used to pen or pencil this may at first seem difficult. But you will soon get used to it and, once you do, will find it adds freedom and spontaneity to your work.

H

HB

2B

It is the most painterly of all drawing instruments. Smudging and erasing charcoal (traditionally done with kneaded pellets of bread) will give far more variety of texture than on a pencil drawing. And any part of the drawing you don't like can be removed with the flick of a rag. Take great care to preserve your successful drawings — by fixing them with a spray fixative (now universally sold in aerosol cans), and by attaching to them an overlay of tissue paper.

Conté crayons, wood-cased or in solid sticks, are available in various degrees of hardness, and in three colours — black, red and white. The cased crayons are easy to sharpen, but the solid sticks are more fun — you can use the side of the stick for large areas of tone. Conté is harder than charcoal, but it is also easy to smudge. The black is very intense.

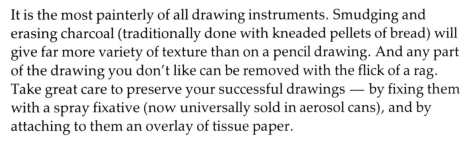

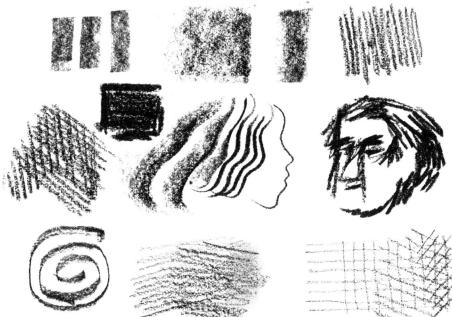

Reed, bamboo and quill pens are good for bold lines. You can make the nib end narrower or wider with the help of a sharp knife or razor blade. This kind of pen has to be dipped frequently into the ink.

Fountain pens have a softer touch than dip-in pens, and many artists prefer them. The portability of a fountain pen makes it a very useful sketching tool.

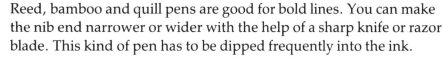

Special fountain pens, such as Rapidograph and Rotring, control the flow of ink by means of a needle valve in a fine tube (the nib). Nibs are available in several grades of fineness and are interchangeable.

The line they produce is of even thickness, but on coarse paper you can draw an interesting broken line similar to that of a crayon. These pens have to be held at a right-angle to the paper, which is a disadvantage.

Inks also vary. Waterproof Indian ink quickly clogs the pen. Pelikan Fount India, which is nearly as black, flows more smoothly and does not leave a varnishy deposit on the pen. Ordinary fountain-pen or writing inks (black, blue, green or brown) are less opaque, so give a drawing more variety of tone. You can mix water with any ink in order to make it even thinner. But if you are using Indian ink, add distilled or rain water, because ordinary water will cause it to curdle.

Ball point pens make a drawing look a bit mechanical, but they are cheap and fool-proof and useful for quick notes and scribbles.

Fibre pens are only slightly better, and (whatever the makers say) their points tend to wear down quickly.

Felt pens are useful for quick notes and sketches, but not good for more elaborate and finished drawings.

Brushes are most versatile drawing instruments. The Chinese and Japanese know this and until recently never used anything else, even for writing. The biggest sable brush has a fine point, and the smallest brush laid on its side provides a line broader than the broadest nib. You can add depth and variety to a pen or crayon drawing by washing over it with a brush dipped in clean water.

Mixed methods are often pleasing. Try making drawings with pen and pencil, pen and wash, charcoal and wash, or Conté and wash. And try drawing with a pen on wet paper. Pencil and Conté do not look well together, and Conté will not draw over pencil or any greasy surface.

Above all, experiment with different techniques, on various qualities and surfaces, even if you quickly find a favourite way of doing things. A new technique will force you to vary the scale of your work and thus see it differently. A small circle, for example, looks different from a large one.

What to draw on

Try as many different surfaces as possible.

Ordinary, inexpensive paper is often as good as anything else: for example, brown and buff wrapping paper (Kraft paper) and lining for wallpaper have surfaces which are particularly suitable for charcoal and soft crayons. Some writing and duplicating papers are best for pen drawings. But there are many papers and brands made specially for the artist.

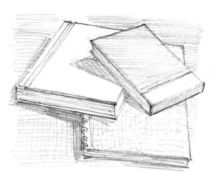

Bristol board is a smooth, hard white board designed for fine pen work.

Ledger Bond ('cartridge' in the UK) the most usual drawing paper, is available in a variety of surfaces — smooth, 'not surface' (semi-rough), rough.

Watercolour papers also come in various grades of smoothness. They are thick, high-quality papers, expensive but pleasant to use.

Ingres paper is mainly for pastel drawings. It has a soft, furry surface and is made in many light colours — grey, pink, blue, buff, etc.

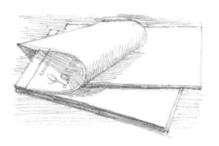

Sketchbooks, made up from nearly all these papers, are available. Choose one with thin, smooth paper to begin with. Thin paper means more pages, and a smooth surface is best to record detail.

Lay-out pads make useful sketchbooks. Although their covers are not stiff, you can easily insert a stiff piece of card to act as firm backing to your drawing. The paper is semi-transparent, but this can be useful — almost as tracing paper — if you want to make a new improved version of your last drawing.

An improvised sketchbook can be just as good as a bought one — or better. Find two pieces of thick card, sandwich a stack of paper, preferably of different kinds, between them and clip together at either end.

Composition

Deciding where to place even the smallest sketch or doodle on a scribbling pad involves composition. The effect of your drawing will be greatly influenced by its position on the paper and by how much space you leave around it.

It is generally best to make you drawing as large as possible on your piece of paper. But there are many possibilities. Sometimes you may not even want the whole of the object on your paper. And there is no reason why the paper should be the same shape as the object — it is not, for instance, necessary to draw a tall object on an upright piece of paper.

When you are drawing more than one object on a sheet of paper, the placing of each object is also important. Try as many variations as possible.

Before you begin a drawing, think about how you will place it on the paper — even a few seconds' thought may save you having to start your drawing again. Never distort your drawing in order to get it all in, or you will wonder why it looks wrong.

Before starting an elaborate drawing, do a few very rough sketches of the main shapes to help you decide on the final composition. When you have decided which to use, rule a faint network of lines — diagonal, vertical and horizontal — over this preliminary sketch and on the piece of paper to be used for the finished drawing. (Take care that both pieces of paper are the same proportion.) You will then have a number of reference points to enable you to transfer the composition to the final drawing.

Rules are made to be broken. Every good artist is a good artist at least partly because of his originality; in fact, because he does what no one else has done before and because he breaks rules.

Every human being is unique. However poor an artist you think you are, you are different from everyone else and your drawing is an expression of your individuality.

Perspective

You can be an artist without knowing anything about perspective. Five hundred years ago, when some of the great masterpieces of all time were painted, the word did not even exist. But most beginners want to know something about it in order to make their drawings appear three-dimensional; so here is a short guide.

The further away an object is, the smaller it seems.

All parallel horizontal lines that are directly opposite you, at right-angles to your line of vision, remain parallel.

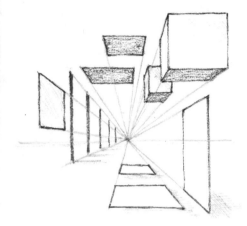

All horizontal lines that are in fact parallel but go away from you will appear to converge at eye-level at the same vanishing point on the horizon. Lines that are above your eye-level will seem to run downwards towards the vanishing point; lines that are below your eye-level will run upwards. You can check the angles of these lines against a pencil held horizontally at eye-level.

The larger and closer any object is, the bigger the front of it will seem to be in relation to the part furthest away, or to any other more distant object. Its actual shape will appear foreshortened or distorted.

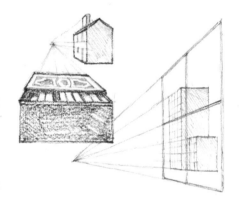

If the side of an object is facing you, one vanishing point is enough; but if the corner is facing you, two vanishing points will be needed.

It may even be necessary to use three vanishing points when your eye is well above or below an object, but these occasions are rare.

Diagonal lines drawn between the opposite angles of a square or rectangle will meet at a point which is half-way along its length or breadth. This remains true when the square or rectangle is foreshortened. You may find it helpful to remember this when you are drawing surfaces with equal divisions — for example, a tiled floor or the divisions between window panes — or deciding where to place the point of a roof or the position of windows on a facade.

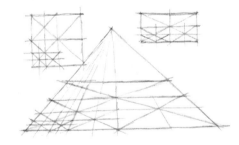

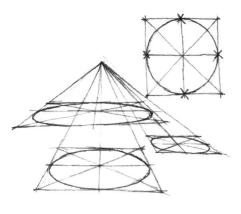

When drawing a circular shape, the following is useful: a circle drawn inside a square will touch the square at the centre point of each of its sides. A foreshortened circle will turn into an oval, but will still touch the centre points of each side of a similarly foreshortened square. However distorted the square, the circle will remain a true oval but will seem to tilt as the square moves to left or right of the vanishing point. The same is true of half circles.

You will tend to exaggerate the apparent depth of top surfaces because you know they are square or rectangular and want to show this in your drawing.

You can check the correct apparent depth of any receding plane by using a pencil or ruler held at eye-level and measuring the proportions on it with your thumb. If you use a ruler you can actually read off the various proportions.

One point to mention again: all receding parallel lines have the same vanishing point. So if, for instance, you draw buildings this will apply to all the horizontal edges — roofs, doors, windows, lines of bricks, chimneys.

The principles of perspective described here, particularly as they apply to boxes and circles, can be helpful when you draw vehicles and trains, as shown on the next four pages and on page 41.

Until well into the 1930s cars were square and box-shaped. But even modern cars can be simplified into a box — and then into two boxes. The wheels can also be inscribed within boxes.

Having established the correctly-proportioned box shapes, refinements such as cutting off the corners, sloping the sides and wind-screen, will give you a realistic rendering of the car.

With a car such as the Mini (right) which is box-like anyhow, the process is even easier and more obvious.

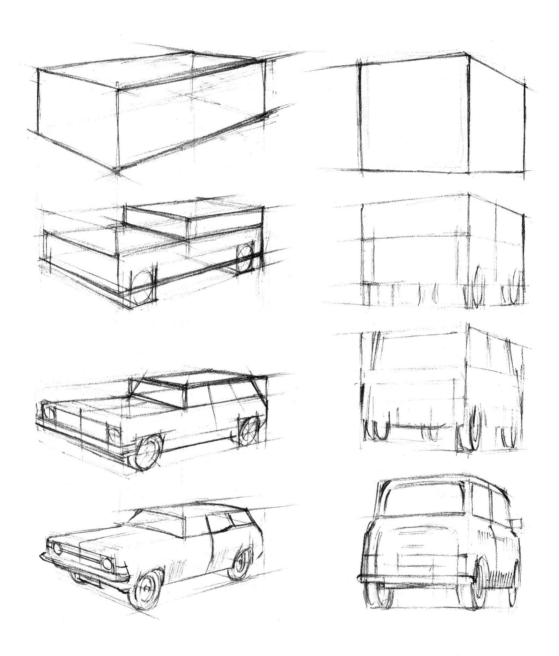

A truck can often be conveniently inscribed within a box, whatever angle it is seen from. Drawn from above, the vanishing point is not at the horizon (eye-level) but below — as it were, underground.

The motor-bike is less easily accommodated in a box, but even here the device can sort out problems of construction. Note that in the second diagram the front wheel, turned to the left, has its own box at an angle to the main structure.

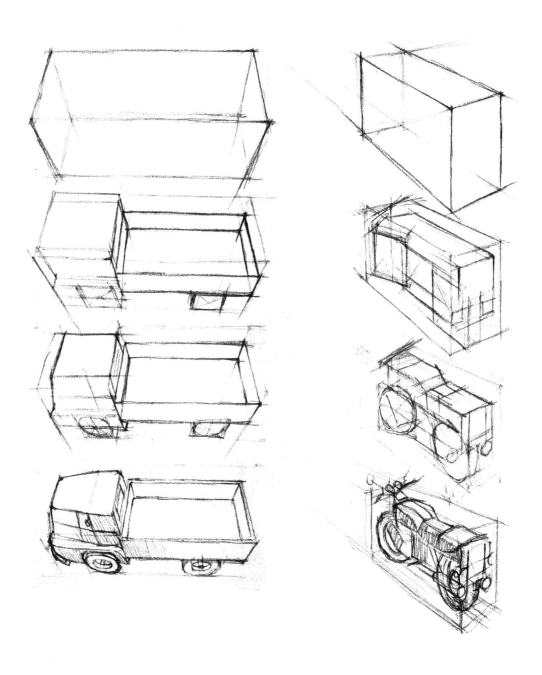

Still using the box-progression, a conventional view of a car is shown on the left. The same car (right) is drawn from a much closer viewpoint and the perspective is therefore exaggerated.

Advertising agents frequently use this effect to present the harmless family saloon as a fierce, powerful and enormous beast.

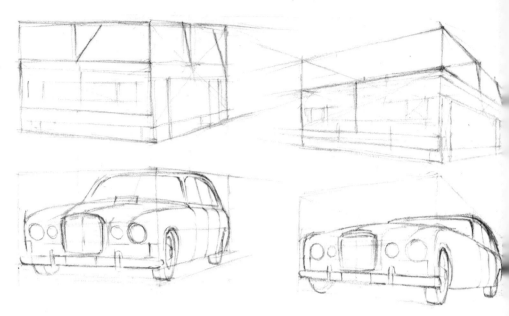

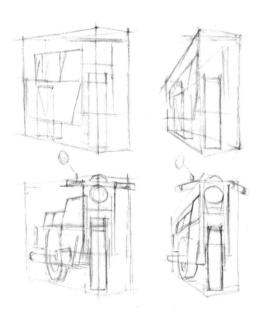

Here the same trick is played with a motor-bike — conventional perspective on the left, exaggerated foreshortening on the right. The front wheel, turned towards you, is seen head on.

As explained earlier, the amount of foreshortening and distortion is determined by the distance you are from an object, rather than its actual size.

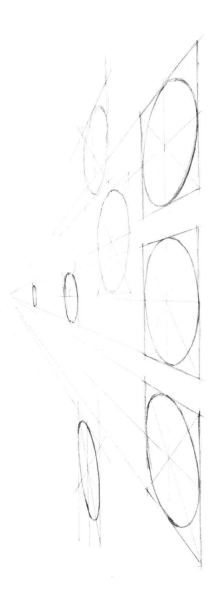

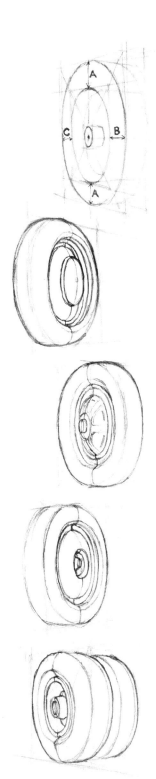

Circles inscribed within foreshortened squares will appear as ellipses with their axes at different angles. The large circle in the middle is a vertical oval; the one above tilts to the right, the one below to the left.

The diagram (top right) explains the apparent differences in wheel thickness. A, top and bottom, is the true depth, B is narrower due to foreshortening, and C, being further from you, appears still smaller.

The drawings of different wheel-trims show how tyre-profile and the dishing and curving of the trim affects the perspective.

However simplified or sketchy your drawing, awareness of these subtleties will give it character and solidity. Look at even the simplest drawings on the next three pages.

Quick
sketches

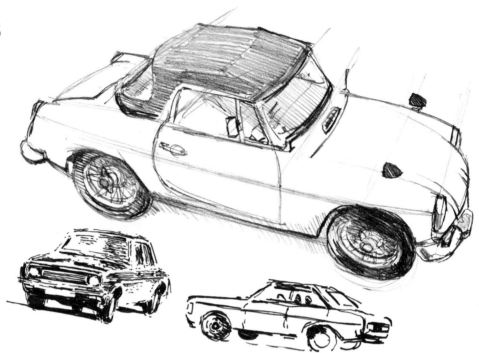

A selection of cars, drawn quickly and simply. The two (lower) drawings, done in a car park, show how grouping can add interest.

Shading is kept to a minimum, mostly to show tonal contrast, as in the first drawing — dark hood and tyres, light body.

The quickest sketches have liveliness and spontaneity at the cost of exact correctness of perspective and detail — a worthwhile exchange.

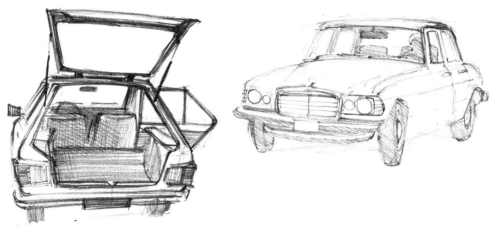

Slightly more careful drawings.

The open doors and back-hatch add interest and an element of the unexpected.

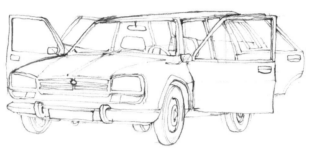

In the drawing below, done with a Rotring pen, modelling and shading start to become important. When going beyond a quick impression, make sure that the direction of the shading is in relation to the shape of the car and follows its curves and mouldings.

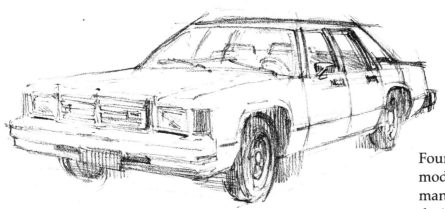

Four current production
models by different
manufacturers share many
design characteristics —
squared headlights,
horizontal emphasis of grill,
similar fenders, curves and
slope of wind-shield and
windows.

The sports car has a more
exciting shape. Using a 2B
pencil (as for the other cars
on this page), I have ignored
detail and stressed the
sculptural shape in simple
black/white contrast.

Heavy vehicles

In these quick drawings I have tried to convey the weight and solidity of trucks and tanker.

The truck with body raised and cab tilted was difficult to draw, but the interesting and unusual shapes made it a worthwhile challenge.

The front wheels of the pick-up in the bottom drawing, turned to the left, appear as circles, whereas the rear wheels are seen foreshortened as ovals.

Bold lines, strong contrast and absence of fuss in this 2B pencil drawing give a sense of the compact strength of tractor and cultivator. Emphasis on the moulded tread of the tyres conveys the firm grip needed to drag the implement through the earth.

Articulated vehicles present a special problem when the towing unit is at an angle to its trailer, as with the dumper truck and trailer, drawn from two different viewpoints. I explain this in more detail when dealing with the perspective of trains on pages 40–43.

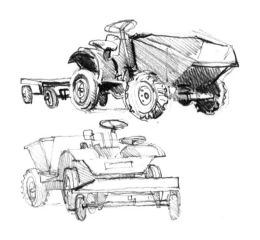

The low viewpoint in this Rotring pen drawing of a large fire-fighting truck gives an impression of size and power. The front wheels are turned to the right so do not conform to the general scheme of perspective.

A miscellany. This and the
two preceding pages also
show a miscellany of
techniques — pencil,
crayon, pen, felt-nib, pen
and crayon combined — and
the unlimited scope for
variety of interpretation.

Truck drawn with chalk and pen in four stages

1 The first chalk lines define main shapes and proportions. Already a few light indications of tone are included.

2 Drawing and shading proceed together. I have extended the drawing into the background. Notice that at any of the first three stages the drawing appears reasonably complete. No part is neglected, or carried much further than any other part.

3 The first pen lines and bold areas of tone appear, deciding the depth of tone to which I could go in the finished drawing.

4 The completed drawing. Tones have been deepened and extended, but the original freshness and freedom has been retained. Detail is not allowed to interfere with the over-all pattern.

Bicycles and motor-bikes

The centre drawing, done from very near the object, is an example of exaggerated perspective (see page 16).

If you include figures, make sure that they do not look like after-thoughts. Notice how, in the bottom left-hand drawing, the rider and his luggage make one shape with the bike.

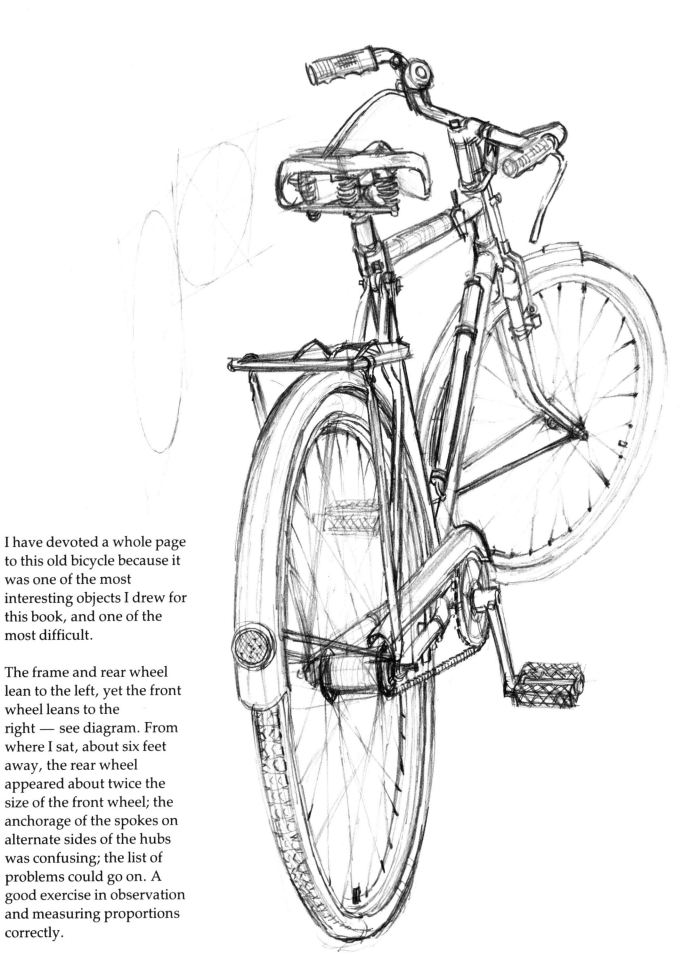

I have devoted a whole page to this old bicycle because it was one of the most interesting objects I drew for this book, and one of the most difficult.

The frame and rear wheel lean to the left, yet the front wheel leans to the right — see diagram. From where I sat, about six feet away, the rear wheel appeared about twice the size of the front wheel; the anchorage of the spokes on alternate sides of the hubs was confusing; the list of problems could go on. A good exercise in observation and measuring proportions correctly.

Pen drawing of motor-bike in three stages

1 The first stage, drawn lightly in pencil, sorts out perspective and proportions and defines the basic structure without any indication of detail.

2 Over this framework the pen is used to establish the main features. Never simply trace over the pencil lines; this would destroy the spontaneity and life of the drawing.

3 The pencil lines are erased, and further detail and tone is added to complete the drawing.

It cannot be stressed enough that the preliminary pencil drawing should not be taken too far. If your confidence allows, it is better to dispense with the pencil sketch altogether. But this may inhibit you and actually make your drawing more timid.

Detail

I have stressed the importance of treating the whole of a vehicle as one unit. But there is also a place for studying and drawing detail. Detail can convey the character, style and period of a vehicle.

The rear fender of the VW Beetle (top left) has, on its own, the sturdiness and bluntness of the whole car and was incidentally quite complicated and difficult to draw.

The pen drawing of the front of a 30-year-old Wolseley saloon makes a good black and white pattern.

The design excesses of the fifties are used in the drawings of rear fins. Here the reflections are as important as the shapes themselves.

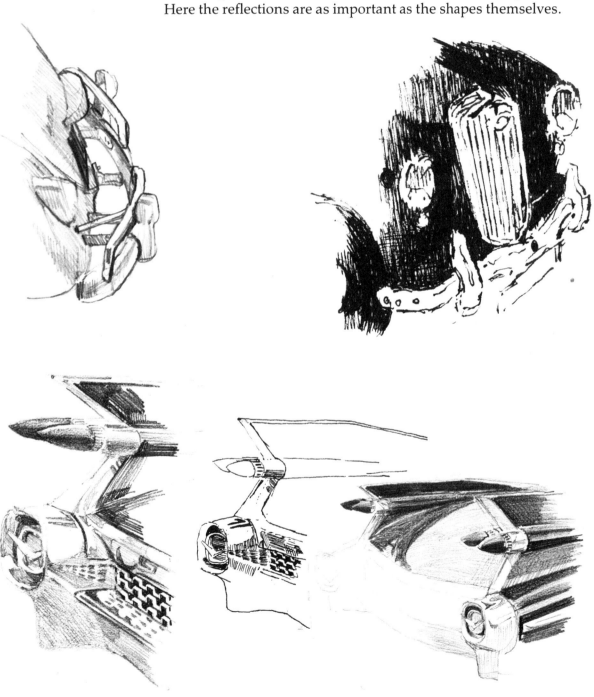

Same car, different techniques

1 HB pencil. A straightforward drawing, conveying in a simple way as much information as possible, such as the difference in texture between chrome grill and fender and the paint-work of the body. Reflections have far more contrast on dark paint-work than on a light body.

2 Fibre pen. Care is taken with the direction and strength of the pen line, making full use of the possible variations in weight — compare the thick lines along the doors with the fine lines on the wind-shield.

3 In contrast, a fine Rotring pen, used scratchily and freely, gives a sense of lightness and movement.

4 Crayon and pen. Using tone as a background demands heavier tones on the car itself, emphasising the contrast of the light areas. This can be taken even further until only white patches stand out on a black background.

Speed

In the first drawing of an ordinary saloon car, the high degree of foreshortening helps the impression of the car rushing towards you.

Speed is suggested by the sports car's shape. The deliberately ill-defined pencil drawing suggests the blurred outline of a fast-moving vehicle.

Similarly, in the pen drawing, the shape of the car and the blurred technique suggest movement.

As in the first drawing, strong foreshortening gives a sense of speed and power to the Formula 1 racing car. The broad chalk treatment also contributes to this.

Here too, sketchy, broad treatment and foreshortening help to convey movement.

Two-wheeled vehicles at speed lean into bends; this is also exploited.

In the groups of cyclists, the similarity of posture of all the riders reinforces the feeling of exertion and speed.

Horizontal lines in background and shadow add to the sense of speed. But beware of the too-obvious device of lines trailing behind car or bike — leave this to the cartoonist or film-animator.

Vintage and veteran cars

Vintage and veteran cars are wonderful subjects. The variety of shapes and the quality of workmanship are an inspiration. To appreciate this fully, draw from the real thing — at rallies and in museums. Photographs are a poor second-best.

Many of these cars still have some of the character of horse-drawn vehicles. Look for instance at the cars at top left and bottom right on this page.

The range from fragility to power, allied to elegance, which these vehicles possess is absent from the modern car.

The carriage (top left) is an example of the vehicles from which the first cars derived their elegance. Notice the dished wheels — the spokes angled inwards to add strength and elasticity.

The black and white treatment of the steam truck was suggested by the white lining on its dark body and wheels.

The lettering all over the vintage truck (bottom left) adds to the interest. Other examples of how trim and lettering can enhance a drawing are the tanker on page 21 and the racing car on page 32.

Groups and settings

Vehicles do not exist in isolation — there is always a setting, a background. However interesting a vehicle may be by itself, it becomes more so in a group and in a setting.

In this B pencil drawing, the all-over linear texture makes a good pattern and conveys the bustle and noise of a busy city. As in the next two drawings, detail and accuracy of perspective are subordinate to the general pictorial atmosphere.

37

A drawing in Rotring pen and chalk of an army convoy in a small town. Here the variety of line and tone suggests movement and the controlled confusion of the scene, for example, in the texture of cobble stones or the detail on tanks and trucks.

Building a modern highway is a massive task requiring large, powerful vehicles and earth-moving machinery, suggested in this crayon drawing by strong, simple lines and by making setting and vehicles part of the same solid pattern. For the larger areas of tone I used a litho crayon on its side. Ink splattered from a stiff brush adds texture.

Trains

Steam engines are more interesting to draw than electric or diesel, so I make no apology for devoting half this section to them.

The first of these two drawings in settings is done with crayon and pen, with a flat grey wash over everything except the white of the steam. White paint is also used for detail.

For the dock-side train I used two widths of line: the tall spidery cranes, drawn with a fine pen, are contrasted with the squat, square shapes of engine and trucks, using a thicker nib. Again, detail is subordinate to atmosphere.

I have already explained the perspective of single vehicles. A train — a chain of vehicles — presents new problems.

1 A train approaching on straight rails: the apparent length of each carriage diminishes rapidly (small diagram, top right).

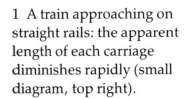

2 A train approaching on an inward curve: each carriage is *less* foreshortened than the preceding one, and each has its own vanishing point — further to the right than the previous one — until the last carriage may, as here, be seen sideways on, in its full length. (See bottom drawing, page 42.)

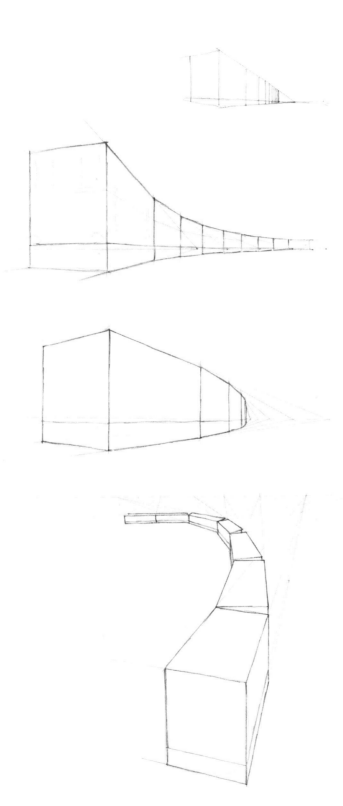

3 A train turning away from you: the first carriage or engine appears longer, with its vanishing point furthest to the right. Each succeeding coach is more foreshortened until they turn out of sight. (See page 40, top, and page 43, bottom.)

4 A curving train seen from above: each segment has two vanishing points — one for the sides, one for the ends. Here, the engine has the vanishing point for the *ends* to the left; but when we get to the third carriage the vanishing point for the *length* is to the left and that for the ends is to the right. The last two carriages are parallel to your view-point and so have only one vanishing point, for the ends.

Turn this diagram upside down to see how to draw a train on a curved overhead track.

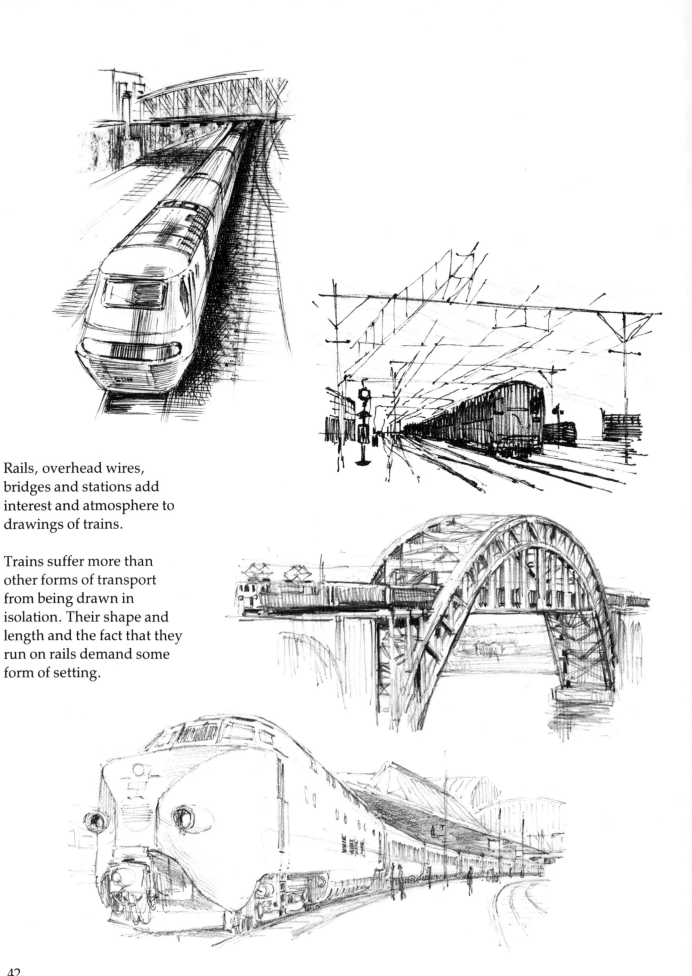

Rails, overhead wires, bridges and stations add interest and atmosphere to drawings of trains.

Trains suffer more than other forms of transport from being drawn in isolation. Their shape and length and the fact that they run on rails demand some form of setting.

In this fibre-pen drawing of a diesel shunting engine, drawn from a distance, there is very little deviation from the horizontal; vanishing points are far out to left and right. I have emphasised the bold black and white of its paint, rather than light and shade.

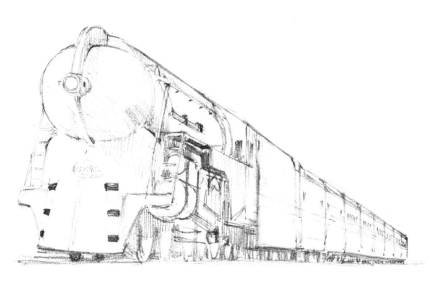

The next two trains are seen in much greater foreshortening. Their perspective is explained on page 41.

This 1930s steam locomotive has the streamlined style associated with cocktail cabinets and movie palaces of the period. The low viewpoint gives this and the next drawing a feeling of power and speed.

Most modern trains have simple, box-like shapes. Character will lie in detail — buffers, suspension, couplings. The low viewpoint emphasises the more interesting areas.

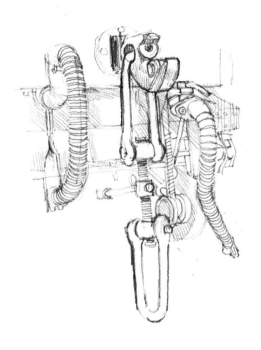

As well as details such as this coupling, objects and buildings connected with railways are good to draw — signals and signal gantries, overhead wires, signal boxes, station buildings, bridges. These two drawings give an idea of the many possibilities.

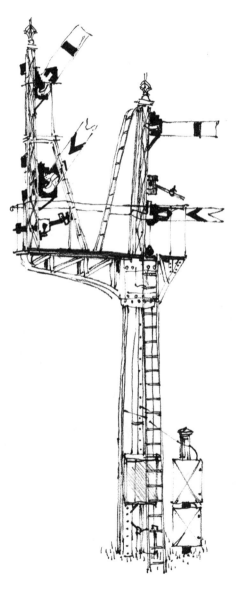

A pencil drawing of Stephenson's 'Rocket', built in 1829

It is tempting to make obsolete machines look quaint and toy-like. I have tried to avoid this by bold and solid treatment, with considerable variety of tone and line.

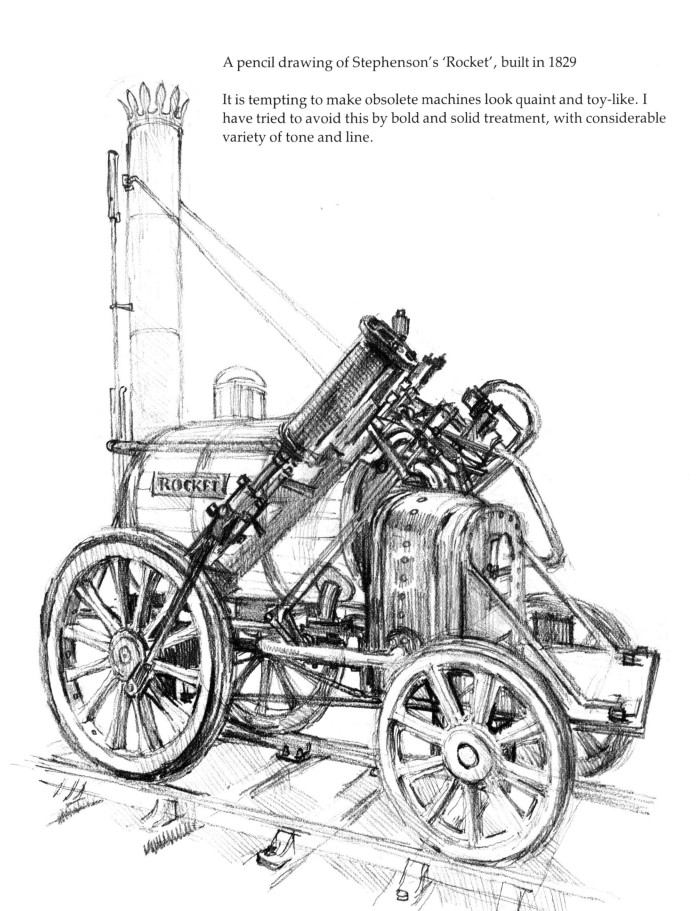

A Rotring pen drawing, using two widths of nib, based on a late-19th-century photograph of owner, manager, foreman and workmen of a loco works posing with their latest product. Instead of trying to disguise the fact that this was drawn from a reference, I have emphasised the awkward stiffness of the posed photo by the scratchy fussiness of the drawing.

Sharp contrast in tone, changes of direction in shading with the fine nib, and variety of texture convey the complicated ruggedness of the locomotive.

A summary of do's and don'ts

This book is only a start. From wheelbarrows to giant excavators, from toy cars to tankers, there is a huge range of vehicles to draw with pleasure and profit.

Draw the parts of a vehicle as well as the whole — dismantled cars, engines, the interiors of cars, buses and trains.

Include the background — the setting in your drawing — in rail stations, bus depots, garages and repair shops, at race meetings, vintage rallies, speed tracks, in the cycle shop, car park, in the street, at the fire station, building sites, airports, museums, the breaker's yard.

Draw the same car, bike, truck from several angles. You will be surprised how much you discover and learn.

Whenever possible, draw from the real thing rather than from a two-dimensional picture. You can choose the angle, the distance, and you will always see more and understand more of the shape and character of your model. A number of drawings in this book are based on photos — but note 'based on', *not* 'copied from'. If you have to use photographic reference, aim for interpretation, not copying.

Never copy other artists' drawings or paintings, not even mine. Look at them, study them, to get hints on technique and interpretation, but don't copy.

Keep your eyes open. Make notes or quick sketches of anything that interests you. Carry a camera too; if there is not time to draw, take a photograph. Let the angle, composition, lighting be *your* choice, not someone else's.

Vary the technique, scale and speed of your drawing. Use pencil, pen, chalk, crayon, brush, charcoal.

If you have a tendency to do small drawings, force yourself to do some big ones — and vice versa.

Do some very quick drawings, no more than five minutes each, one after the other.

Now and then, spend as much time as possible on one drawing.

As a general rule, look carefully and slowly, draw freely and quickly.

Discard drawings ruthlessly if they go wrong. Don't mess about with them, start again.

Finally, draw, draw and draw. The more you draw, the better you draw, and the more personal your work will become.